How to Build a Work Breakdown Structure

The Cornerstone of Project Management

Carl L. Pritchard

ESI International
Arlington, VA

Published by

ESI International
4301 Fairfax Drive
Arlington, Virginia 22203

©1998 by ESI International

Printed in the United States of America
ISBN 1-890367-12-5

Contents

About the Author v

About ESI International vii

Acknowledgments ix

Chapter 1: Introduction 1
  What *is* a Work Breakdown Structure? 1

Chapter 2: Mechanics of the WBS 5
  Numerical Sequencing 5
    Top Level 5
    Second Level 5
    Third Level and Beyond 5
  WBS Orientation 6
    Deliverable Orientation 6
    Task Orientation 9
  WBS Construction Approach 13
    Top-Down Deliverable 14
      Top-Down Deliverable WBS Checklist 16
    Top-Down Task 17
      Top-Down Task-Oriented WBS Checklist 19
    Bottom-Up Task 20
      Bottom-Up Task-Oriented WBS Checklist 22
    Filling the Gaps 23
      Networking 23
        Networking Applicability Checklist 24
        Networking Approach Checklist 26
      Delphi Technique 27
        Delphi Technique Applicability Checklist 28
      Consultant Validation 29
        Consultant Validation Applicability Checklist 30
      Template Comparison 30
    Template Construction 31
      Meeting the Customer's Needs 32
      Template Checklist 37
    Hybrids 38
      The Living, Growing WBS 39

Chapter 3: Communicating WBS Changes 43
    Version Control Checklist 47
Chapter 4: Closing Out the WBS 49
    Storage and Retrieval.. 51
Appendix A—Idea-Generation Techniques for Designing
An Effective WBS.. 53
    Brainstorming 53
    Crawford Slip.. 53
    Nominal Group Technique (NGT)... 54
    Others 55
Index 57

About the Author

Carl Pritchard is the principal of Pritchard Management Associates and is a recognized project management speaker, author, instructor, and course designer. His recent projects include *Risk Management: Concepts and Guidance, Managing Projects in Organizations, The CD-ROM* with David Frame, and a chapter in the *Field Guide to Project Management*, edited by David Cleland. He was the principal architect of ESI International's acclaimed distance learning program in project management. He writes and presents on topics ranging from presentation techniques to strategic project management.

Mr. Pritchard is active in professional project management associations and is a certified Project Management Professional (PMP[*]). He earned a B.A. in journalism from The Ohio State University.

Mr. Pritchard lives in Frederick, Maryland, with his wife, Nancy, and two sons, Adam and James.

---

[*] PMP is a registered Certification Mark of the Project Management Institute, Inc.

About ESI International

ESI International is a training and consulting firm founded as Educational Services Institute in 1981. For the past 17 years, our professionals have helped other professionals acquire knowledge and competencies in contract management, nonprofit and public administration management, global business management, and project management.

Our one-of-a-kind curriculum has become the world's premier professional development program in project management. Tens of thousands of professionals from around the world have benefited from seven core courses and dozens of electives leading to Master's Certificates in either Project Management or Information Technology Project Management from The George Washington University. In 1996 alone, we presented 1- to 5-day sessions to nearly 28,000 attendees on six continents. We also develop and teach tailored sessions as requested by many of the world's largest corporations in diverse industries, such as telecommunications, oil exploration and refining, financial services, and computer manufacturing.

ESI provides a variety of project management consulting services ranging from individual and organizational assessments, to methodology development, to hands-on coaching and mentoring.

Call 1-703-558-3020 for a catalog, or visit our Web site at http://www.esi-intl.com.

Acknowledgments

I put together this book as a "first effort" in a new phase of my longstanding relationship with ESI. My thanks to the management team, especially *Nick Schacht, Larry Seeley, LeRoy Ward,* and *Jerry Mazzuchi,* as they provided the opportunity for me to expand my opportunities to advance the profession through writing. Thanks also to *Deborah Brissman* and *Godfrey Parkin* for picking up the distance learning efforts to free me for this endeavor. A special thanks to *Angela Weaver,* who pushed constantly to ensure the quality and schedule constraints were met. Also, thanks to *Trinh Le* for her word processing help.

The book represents not only my thinking, but that of thousands of students I've encountered in the ESI classroom, who deserve recognition for their individual commitments to better project management practice. I appreciate their contributions more than they will ever realize.

My unending gratitude goes also to my wife, *Nancy* and sons, *Adam* and *James,* for their love, patience, support, and supply of Mountain Dew® as this book was crafted.

Chapter 1

Introduction

Surprisingly little has been written about the mechanics of crafting a work breakdown structure (WBS). While project managers are consistently expected to create the WBS as the cornerstone of their project plans, there are limited references on how to actually go about crafting one that works. Instead, managers document project activities and deliverables using their own intuition and experiences, or they resort to their organization's set practices and procedures.

Here, we will provide you with different approaches to WBS construction and will highlight the advantages and disadvantages of each of these approaches. We will also examine the implications of the different styles of WBS and the level of depth that your project requires.

What *is* a Work Breakdown Structure?

Even the definition of a WBS is up for discussion. The Project Management Institute's *Guide to the Project Management Body of Knowledge (PMBOK)* defines the WBS *as a **deliverable**-oriented* [emphasis added] *grouping of project elements which organizes and defines the total scope of the project. Each descending level represents an increasingly detailed definition of a project component. Project components may be products or services.*[1] This is a somewhat radical shift from the PMBOK definition of just a few years ago, where the WBS was described as *a **task**-oriented* [emphasis added] *family tree of activities which organizes, defines, and graphically displays the total work to be accomplished in order to achieve the final objectives of a project.*[2] Some books describe the WBS as a visual model generated by

---

[1] *Guide to the Project Management Body of Knowledge*, PMI Standards Committee, Project Management Institute, PA, 1996.

[2] *Project Management Body of Knowledge*, Project Management Institute, PA, 1987.

the project team,[3] while others refer to it as a hierarchical task list with a logical structure.[4] The definitions take in a broad range of perspectives, possibilities, and opinions. For the sake of this discussion, we will attempt to address the practical application of the WBS by defining it only as a decomposition of the work to be performed that is arranged in a hierarchy and constructed to allow for clear logical grouping of the tasks to be performed or the deliverables to be provided.

Essentially, the WBS serves as the framework for project plan development. Much like the frame of a house, it supports all basic components as they are developed and built. And, much like the frame of a house, it can be considered complete at different stages by different parties. For those pouring concrete, the frame is essentially complete when the footers are in place. For those responsible for putting shingles on the roof, it will be a long time before they consider the framework done. Similarly, for those responsible at the task level, the work breakdown structure is complete only when their tasks are defined.

In building the WBS, various parties involved in its construction must be aware of its depth and scope. They need to know how large it will be, when it will be deemed complete, and what their roles are. If they are responsible only at a high level, they should be aware that the lower levels will be added later. The same is true for team members at the lower levels of the WBS. Project managers should not, however, be tempted to create work breakdown structures so detailed that team members are inhibited from independent thought. An old saying among project managers emphasizes that a WBS is too detailed when it tells team members, "Move Left Foot, Move Right Foot."

---

[3] *Field Guide to Project Management*, Cleland, David, editor, Van Nostrand Reinhold, NY, 1998, p.74.

[4] *Project Management: How to Plan and Manage Successful Projects*, Joan Knutson & Ira Bitz, AMACOM, 1995, p. 4.

Before we get into the specifics, we will examine important points that are crucial to building a useful and powerful WBS.

As a critical tool in project planning, an effective WBS should be used in different ways to serve various project needs.

Chapter 2

Mechanics of the WBS

Numerical Sequencing

Top Level

Regardless of the approach, the work breakdown structure (WBS) looks fundamentally the same. The top level, or project level, is 1.0. This convention allows us to know that everything labeled 1.x is associated with this project. In some organizations, a number is assigned to the project. Thus, when a project is assigned, its top level may be 18 or 145. This allows for tracking of the projects within larger organizational programs and allows for better historical tracking of projects.

Second Level

The second level will carry the same first digit, followed by a decimal point, then another set of integers starting with one. Thus, under Level 1.0, the second level would have groups subcomponents 1.1, 1.2, 1.3, etc. Level 1.0 rarely is the lowest level of the work breakdown structure (save for the most rudimentary educational examples). In virtually all work breakdown structures, this is the reporting or summary level. It summarizes all of the work that fall within its scope in the structure and provides a tracking mechanism for all activities that fall under it.

Third Level and Beyond

The third level will carry the same first two sets of digits, a decimal point, then another set of integers. Thus, the third level would have subcomponents 1.1.1, 1.1.2, 1.1.3, and so on.

This effort continues down until we have a numerical hierarchy for the entire project. When we're done, we can identify the relationships among activities by their numerical sequencing alone, since we know that activity

2.6.77.3 is a part of Project #2, second level summary activity or deliverable #6, and so forth.

WBS Orientation

The lowest level of the WBS, where the work is actually assigned, is known as the work package (discussed later). The level above the work package is a reporting level (used for all management reporting, not just financial reports) known as the cost account.

Some sample work breakdown structures are provided below. For these examples, two different orientations of the information are presented. These two orientations are significant in that the project manager needs to determine which approach will serve the best interests of the project. The choices are between task- and deliverable-oriented WBS. Many of the greatest disagreements on WBS use stem from whether it should support the task structure or the deliverables on the project. Both sides in the disagreement consider themselves purists in project management, although the prevailing schools of thought side with a deliverables orientation.

Deliverable Orientation

In the WBS below, note that the elements at the highest level are deliverables associated with this project. As the work is broken down, subcomponents of the primary deliverables are described. This continues down to the lowest levels of the WBS, where the work is defined by simple, easy-to-understand and easy-to-manage deliverables that are the responsibility of a single individual, a single organization, or a single function within the organization.

Note that the activities here are all clearly focused on the deliverable above them. The orientation is not by phase, or by checkpoints, but by the deliverables that have to be produced. Under a single deliverable, it is reasonable to assume that there may be activities ranging from the first day of the project to the last. There is very little orientation toward the timing of the components. Instead, the orientation is on the components themselves.

In opting for the deliverables orientation, there are some distinct advantages and disadvantages. With this approach, the organization effectively tracks its costs associated with particular deliverables and is able to use comparative or analogous estimating. It rewards teams and projects based on the quality of deliverables and their components and records what's been accomplished, who accomplished the work, and how quality on a single component or subcomponent was achieved.

This approach is not without its downside. Team members accustomed to listing WBS activities based on their sequence in the project may find it hard to understand, much less build, a deliverable-oriented WBS. In addition, the deliverables-oriented WBS does not show the activities common to two or more deliverables and how these activities interrelate in nature, scope, and resource requirements—information valuable in tracking and evaluating the project.

The question remains—will this approach help the customer, the team, and the organization track the project both now and for future use?

Let's use the simple example of an office move. Here, the target deliverable is the organization's completed move to a new facility. To accomplish that goal, the organizers have identified the key deliverables as the efforts to (1) move networks, (2) move equipment, and (3) move personnel:

1.0   Organizational Move

     1.1   Network Move
     1.2   Equipment Move
     1.3   Personnel Move

Under Network Move, there could be several key deliverables:

     1.1   Network Move

         1.1.1   Server Move
         1.1.2   Backup Systems Move
         1.1.3   Workstation Move

Under Workstation Move, there could be a breakdown either by office group or by other pertinent deliverables.

1.1.3   Workstation Move

1.1.3.1   Word Processing Workstation Move
1.1.3.2   Data Entry Workstation Move
1.1.3.3   Customer Service Workstation Move

If those departments are sufficiently large, there might even be cause to break the deliverables down even further.

1.1.3.2   Data Entry Workstation Move

1.1.3.2.1   Sun Workstation Transfer
1.1.3.2.2   M/S Workstation Transfer
1.1.3.2.3   Mac Workstation Transfer

Note that each level is identified not by the work performed, but by the deliverable. Even among supporters of the deliverables-oriented WBS, there are different schools of thoughts associated with the lowest level of the WBS—the work package. One school of thought argues that since the rest of the WBS focuses on deliverables, the work package should do the same, as in the example above. The other school of thought argues that the lowest level of the WBS should always feature a "verb-object" or task orientation to describe the specific work that has to be accomplished. The latter approach is more specific in describing these work packages—the lowest level of the WBS—and how they should be accomplished.

A classic story came from a telecommunications project manager who, during a WBS review, could not identify what actual work was expected from an activity labeled "Transportation." He knew transportation (whatever it was) was the ultimate deliverable, but he didn't know what had to be transported. If the activity had been named "Transport Switcher," he would have been able to readily identify the activity and justify the costs. The verb-object orientation at the lowest (work package) level ensures some modicum of clarity on what work is being done. For the example above, the work package level could be modified as follows:

1.1.3.2   Data Entry Workstation Move

1.1.3.2.1   Transfer Sun Workstation to New Facility
1.1.3.2.2   Transfer M/S Workstation to New Facility
1.1.3.2.3   Transfer Mac Workstation to New Facility

It doesn't change the nature of the activities, only the way in which they are expressed. Deliverables-oriented purists believe that this orientation makes it more difficult to report on the specific deliverables that have been produced.

Task Orientation

While the deliverable-oriented WBS has become the predominant approach over the past few years, the task-oriented WBS remains a favorite among project managers whose projects are heavily time-dependent and whose organizations are steadfast in their orientation toward "checkpoints" and "gates" that allow for progress from stage to stage or phase to phase. Task-oriented work breakdown structures break the work out by task groupings that either occur within the same timeframe or are related in function. In the sample WBS, note that work relating to similar deliverables may stretch across different subsets of the structure. It's wholly conceivable that a single deliverable could have activity in the 1.1, 1.2, 1.3, *and* 1.4 levels.

It's much more challenging to track the progress of a single component in a task-oriented WBS as its components may be scattered across the structure. In process-oriented projects—reorganizations, business process reengineering—the process is far more important than the deliverables involved.

On the other hand, task-oriented WBS has the advantage of facilitating schedules and clarifying cross-component or cross-functional relationships as they apply within a given phase or set of tasks.

In using the same example we used for the deliverables-oriented WBS, the only change has been to reflect a time-scaled (or checkpoint-scaled) orientation.

      1.0   Move to New Facility
            1.1   Concept Phase
            1.2   Development Phase
            1.3   Implementation Phase
            1.4   Termination Phase

Organizations have varying rules about how projects should progress from checkpoint to checkpoint or phase to phase. In some cases, the organization may dictate that progress on the Development Phase cannot begin until *all* of the steps in the Concept Phase are complete. Others dictate that some preliminary steps be accomplished before it's possible to move forward to the next checkpoint. Organizations that use these approaches to project management are often compelled to adhere to the task-oriented approach to WBS construction.

As you progress down the WBS, the activities are grouped by tasks, rather than by deliverables. In this example, the Implementation Phase might include all work done by a single group of specialists:

    1.3   Implementation Phase

        1.3.1   Move Workstations
        1.3.2   Move Office Equipment
        1.3.3   Move Personal Effects

You may note that the same work is being accomplished, but the orientation is different. The various subsets that were at the 1.x level in the deliverable-oriented example have been relegated to the 1.x.x level here. Strangely enough, when it gets down to the lowest levels, there's an eerie sameness between the approaches:

        1.1.4   Move Workstations

            1.1.4.4   Move Word Processing Workstations
            1.1.4.5   Move Data Entry Workstations
            1.1.4.6   Move Customer Service Workstations

And again one level deeper:

        1.1.4.2   Move Data Entry Workstations

            1.1.4.2.1   Transfer Sun Workstation to New Facility
            1.1.4.2.2   Transfer M/S Workstation to New Facility

1.1.4.2.3 Transfer Mac Workstation to New Facility

Which approach is right? Different organizations have different practices and oftentimes it is difficult to take an outsider's view on what the appropriate approach should be. Bottom line: the approach you select should mirror your organization's culture and your organization's needs.

If there is no set procedure for implementing work breakdown structures in your organization, this checklist will help you determine the type of WBS most appropriate for your project. As with any generic checklist, it is not infallible, but it will provide some degree of accuracy in your selection process.

Question	Rationale	Deliverable-Oriented WBS	Task-Oriented WBS
Is project progress measured by deliverables?	Some organizations receive payment based on deliverables or track performance based on deliverables.	Y	N
Is the project tracked by time-oriented checkpoints?	Some organizations receive payment based on their ability to meet a series of objective criteria at the beginning or end of a phase.	N	Y
Is cost considered a bigger issue than time?	Effective cost tracking is a key feature of the deliverable-oriented WBS.	Y	N
Does the organization like to track costs against phases?	It's very challenging to track phase-by-phase costs in a deliverable-oriented WBS.	N	Y
Are multiple functional organizations responsible for each deliverable?	If so, and if the functions want to know their relative contributions to the project, those contributions will be easier to reflect in a task-oriented WBS.	N	Y
Do deliverables and functional organizations tend to align?	In this situation, the deliverable orientation allows for clear reporting back to the functional groups.	Y	N

Question	Rationale	Deliverable-Oriented WBS	Task-Oriented WBS
Will the entire team contribute to the WBS? Will much of that development be concurrent?	Using the whole team to build the WBS is a positive experience, but it tends to lead to a linear, rather than compartmentalized, perspective on how activities should be grouped.	N	Y
Will large elements of the WBS be constructed in relative isolation by subject matter experts?	Subject matter experts are best left to organize their thoughts in the logical groupings they understand. They will likely best understand their own deliverables.	Y	N
Are WBS templates in place for the deliverables or components?	Organizational methodologies should take precedence over personal preference. The inverse is true here as well. If there are templates for a task orientation, that should be the default.	Y	N
Have we built the components before but are using a new way to bring them together?	It's vital to build on experience. If there are significant sections of the WBS which can be drawn from lessons learned, they should be deployed.	Y	N
Is this a highly experimental, build-as-you-go approach?	When deliverables change from week to week or month to month, it is useless predicting which deliverables will ultimately survive the process.	N	Y

While this checklist doesn't cover every possible parameter, it offers important considerations when choosing the appropriate WBS. In addition, consider the culture of the organization. A change in approach may be worthwhile only if it will make tracking significantly easier and improve customer understanding.

Whether it's task-oriented or deliverable-oriented, the question is: "How do you actually build a work breakdown structure?"

WBS Construction Approach

As the title of this section implies, there are a variety of ways to tackle WBS construction. Some have a greater history than others. Some are considered avant-garde while others are perceived as passé. It's important not to dismiss any of them. At one time or another, on some project or another, they worked, and they worked extremely well. Otherwise, they wouldn't have made it into popular thinking.

For a time, PMI espoused the seven-level WBS. Project management author and researcher Harold Kerzner recommended a six-level approach,[5] while others felt the WBS should be more fluid. Most popular thought now rests with the last group.

The WBS today tends to reflect the depth necessary to get the work done. If the customer demands extensive reporting on a particular type of activity or set of deliverables, the WBS should facilitate that reporting. It should also reflect the degree of control the project manager need. For his part, the project manager should ask how much information will be required at each of those levels to truly manage the work. As a tool, the WBS should support the PM, the project, the customer, and the team.

There was, however, an advantage to the predetermined levels that were established under the older schools of thought. That advantage stems from clear labels associated with each of the levels. You knew what each level was supposed to incorporate and how information was to be sorted. That eliminated some of the latent "flip-flopping" project managers are compelled to do when they're building the WBS from scratch. In Kerzner's model, for example, the six levels were program, project, task, subtask, work package, level of effort. In PMI's version, the work package is considered the lowest level of the WBS and the place where work is actually assigned. In any case, the predetermined levels afforded project managers some insight on *what* information was to be included *where*.

The downside of using predetermined levels in a work breakdown structure is that it often forces project managers to a level of detail the project does not require. A seven-level work breakdown structure applied on a smaller

---

[5] *Project Management: A Systems Approach to Planning, Scheduling and Control, Fourth Edition*, Kerzner, Harold, Van Nostrand Reinhold, NY, 1992, p. 609

project would give us this description for the lowest level: 1.1.2.4.5.6.2 – Move Left Foot. This level of detail is simply unnecessary.

The main goal is to break down the project into major work packages that, in turn, can be divided into specific tasks and subtasks. In addition, each work package should be assignable so that accountability can be expected and used as a measure for monitoring the project's status. The key is choosing the approach that enables the organization to implement the within the specified schedule, cost, and to performance objectives.

The WBS construction approaches we will examine in depth here are:

- Top-Down Deliverable,
- Top-Down Task,
- Bottom-Up Task,
- Template, and
- Hybrids

For each of the construction approaches, there will be a series of questions to assist you in constructing the documentation at the end of the section.

Top-Down Deliverable

This approach is perhaps the most common and the most widely accepted of those currently in practice. As the name implies, it is deliverable-oriented. That means the top level of the WBS—the first level you will define—will be the name of the overall project deliverable. That name should be the widely accepted name of the project deliverable and should be readily recognizable to the customer and to the project team members and stakeholders. That level will be given the first integer label (e.g., 1.0 or 34.0).

The next level of the top-down deliverable WBS will be the key component level. These are the key components of the project deliverable (already defined at the top level). If you were building a computer, these components might include the monitor, the motherboard, the hard drive, the DVD drive, and other components that make up the computer. The key components should include all the major elements of the computer. Everything, from the shell to the modem to the internal cables and wires will have to fit within one of those components. On the general level, WBS components identified at this level should also include all the major elements of the deliverable. While it's not unreasonable to have lesser components at this level, it's a good idea to identify and group elements of equal importance to create a balance in the WBS. The key component level will be identified by a single integer (from the project level) followed by the identifying number assigned at this level (e.g., 1.1, 1.2, 1.3, and so on).

At this level, it's important to ensure that you have not forgotten any of what may now seem like the lesser issues associated with the deliverable. Failure to identify all elements may cause tasks to go either unidentified or unaccounted for in the final WBS. It's also important to ensure, at this point, that you have a clear perspective on how deep your WBS should ultimately go. If you are determined to complete the WBS in only three or four levels, you may be forced to begin broadening your perspective at this point.

Your decisions here may depend on customer demands. If the customer requires reports on only key components, you may wish to use the customer reporting strategy to determine which elements will be included at this level.

Beyond the key component level, there can be a virtually infinite number of subcomponent levels, depending upon the magnitude of the deliverables. Someone defining the deliverables for a desktop computer will deal with far fewer subcomponents and far fewer levels than the individual defining deliverables for a commercial airplane. To determine the level of depth that's appropriate, the project manager needs to examine the relative number and complexity of the components that are being defined. A WBS level that requires three-digit numbers to cover all of the deliverables (subcomponents) at that level is probably too broad. Better to narrow the number of subcomponents by broadening the definition of what they are. If a massive computer had 35 different types of data storage (along with all of the other components), better to group them together as "Data Storage Devices" than to list each device separately at one level, along with all of the other project subcomponents. When your list of deliverables at any given level grows to several dozen, it may be time to re-evaluate the deliverables to identify a more logical grouping of the deliverables as a single subcomponent.

As discussed earlier, this effort continues until we break down the work so that all team members can understand either the work that's to be done or the products that are to be delivered.   At the lowest level, the project manager must ultimately make the determination whether the work packages will be expressed as "verb-object" tasks or as low-level deliverables (or sub-subcomponents).

If the project manager wants to clarify tasks for team members, the verb-object approach provides a more direct description of information. If upper management holds the project manager accountable on a deliverable-by-deliverable basis, a deliverables orientation is probably more appropriate at this level.

Top-Down Deliverable WBS Checklist

1.   What is the overall deliverable of this project? Insert this item at the 1.0 level of your WBS.

Success Criteria: Is the definition of the deliverable clear to all parties concerned? Do the key stakeholders agree on the nature of the deliverable?

2.   Have you identified the key components of this project? Assign each of them a number and precede it with the 1.0 integer assigned under question #1.

Success Criteria: Do your key components encompass *everything* that will ultimately comprise the project deliverable? Are the deliverables of roughly the same scope?

3.   For each component, have you identified its *major* subcomponents? Assign each of them a number and precede it with the 1.x integer assigned under question #2.

Success Criteria: Do the subcomponents work together to comprise all of the aspects of the key components? Has nothing been omitted? Are the deliverables of roughly the same scope? Are there fewer than several dozen major subcomponents? If not, are the subcomponents still of such a critical nature and magnitude that they must be expressed at this level and cannot logically be grouped together?

4.   For the remaining subcomponent levels, have you repeated Step #3 down to a level where the deliverables are now sufficiently small and

manageable so that they can be accomplished by the team at a level of control that you can oversee effectively?

Success Criteria: Are the subcomponents sufficiently decomposed to allow for clear understanding of all of the elements of the project? Have all of the deliverables in the project been accounted for?

5.   At the work package level, has the work been defined to the point where the components or activities at the lowest level are readily understood by those doing the work? Can the work be accomplished in a timeframe and at a cost proportionate to the other activities at this level?

Success Criteria: Does a brief survey of team members indicate they understand their deliverables and how they contribute to the whole project? Do team members know their assigned work? Are all activities roughly the same magnitude in terms of cost and duration?

Top-Down Task

The top-down task approach to WBS development is similar to the deliverables-oriented approach, with one key distinction. The thinking here is always oriented toward the activities to be accomplished and the work to be done, rather than on the deliverables that are to be produced. This tends to be a far more linear approach to project management and is often the result of organizations that have established time-focused or checkpoint-driven project management methodologies or approaches.

This approach is second only to top-down deliverable in its level of use. Most project managers use one form of top-down WBS development (unless their organizations already have templates or samples from which to build the WBS). In a top-down task WBS, the top level is, as the name implies, task-oriented. The top level of the WBS—the first level you will define— will be the name of the overall project goal. That goal should be brief and clear because it will serve as the project's name. It also should be readily recognizable to the customer and to the project team members and stakeholders. That level will be given the first integer label (e.g., 1.0 or 42.0).

The next level of the top-down task WBS is the phase, checkpoint, or gate-keeping level. This level is designed to provide a dismantling of the work across a timeline. Different organizations often have predetermined levels here. The *Guide to the PMBOK* recognizes no fewer than five different life cycles,[6] and the phases or steps associated with each of these could easily serve as a component of the WBS. In this approach, the generic life-cycle labels of Concept, Development, Implementation, and Termination serve as the "children" to the "parent" activity at the project level. At this level, elements of the WBS are given the second integer label (e.g., 1.1 or 42.3).

Continuing down the structure, the task-oriented WBS now has a number of summary levels. These levels continue the process of decomposing the work based, in large part, on its position in the project timeline. In short, *when* the work is going to happen is more important than *what* is going to be produced in the process. Frequently, the timing of the work and the nature of the work blur at this level, making it look similar to (if not identical to) a deliverable-oriented WBS from this point on. The key difference is that the emphasis here is on summarizing the work (tasks) at lower levels rather than on gathering together elements of a single subcomponent deliverable. As an example, the Implementation Phase for a home construction project could easily be subdivided into summary activities including Slab Preparation, Frame Construction, and Roof Construction. While each of these focuses on a specific deliverable, they are equally significant in that they mark progress across the timeline and are often used as time-oriented milestones in a construction project. The slab is poured and cured before the frame is built, and the frame is constructed before a roof can be mounted.

There can be a series of summary levels, depending upon the complexity of the project and the overall project duration. Note that overall project duration—not the number of components and subcomponents—becomes a more critical factor in the task-oriented WBS. That's because the orientation is on tasks, rather than deliverables (although the end result is the same). To determine how many summary levels of depth are appropriate, the project manager needs to take a look at the volume of work and the timeframes being defined. A WBS level that grows to three-digit numbers to encompass all of the summaries (at a given level) is too expansive. One easy way to evaluate if work at this level needs to be further subdivided is by evaluating

---

[6] *Guide to the Project Management Body of Knowledge,* PMI Standards Committee, Project Management Institute, PA, 1996.

its overall impact on the phase level. If a single summary activity (Build Frame) is disproportionately large compared to the other summaries, then it should be broken down further. In the inverse, if a summary activity represents work at such a micro level that it is either too detailed or cannot be decomposed further, it may not be appropriate at this level. It may actually be a component of some other summary activity. (The task "Mix Concrete" may not warrant its own summary, but may instead belong as a subset of Concrete Preparation, which is a subset of Slab Preparation).

The decomposition continues until we break down the work to a level of detail where all team members can understand either the work that is to be done or the products that are to be delivered. At the lowest level, the task-oriented WBS is highlighted by tasks to be performed, normally expressed as verb-object work packages.

Top-Down Task-Oriented WBS Checklist

1. What is the overall deliverable of this project? Insert this item at the 1.0 level of your WBS.

Success Criteria: Is the definition of the deliverable clear to all parties concerned? Do the key stakeholders agree on the nature of the deliverable?

2. Have you identified the key phases or life-cycle steps of this project? Assign each of them a number and precede it with the 1.0 integer assigned under question #1.

Success Criteria: Do your key phases or life-cycle steps encompass the entire duration of the project? Do they include all activities involved to produce the final project deliverable? Are the phases or steps either pre-determined by the organization, or do they represent a logical and readily accepted flow of progress?

3. For each phase, have you identified logical groupings of work which summarize the activity below them? Assign each of them a number and precede it with the 1.x integer assigned under question #2.

Success Criteria: Do the summaries work together to comprise all of the aspects of the phases, checkpoints or life-cycle steps? Do the summaries have the same scope? Are there fewer than several dozen major summaries?

If not, are the summaries of work still of such a critical nature and magnitude that they must be expressed at this level and cannot logically be grouped together?

4. For the remaining summary levels, have you repeated Step #3 down to a level where the summaries of work are now sufficiently small and manageable so that they can be accomplished by the team at a level of control that you can oversee effectively?

Success Criteria: Are the summaries sufficiently decomposed to allow for clear understanding of all of the work on the project? Has the entire project timeline been accounted for?

5. At the work package level, has the work been defined to the point where the components or activities at the lowest level are readily understood by those doing the work? Can the work be accomplished in a timeframe and at a cost proportionate to the other activities at this level?

Success Criteria: Does a brief survey of team members indicate they understand their deliverables and their individual contribution to the project? Do team members know what is expected of them? Are all activities roughly the same magnitude in terms of cost and duration?

Bottom-Up Task

The bottom-up task development approach to WBS construction works best in an environment where the team members have a clear sense of the work in particular but are unclear on how they fit together or if they have *all* of the activities clearly defined. In high-performing teams in highly developmental projects, identifying the deliverables or the summaries may be too onerous. In organizations where the WBS is an unfamiliar tool, the thought of slogging through the formality of the WBS structure can be intimidating.

In a bottom-up task-oriented WBS, the construction of the structure begins not at the top level, but (as the name implies) at the bottom. In order to properly develop a bottom-up WBS, all of the key personnel responsible for project work need to be present. The project manager begins with a clear explanation that the objective is to simply identify all of the work necessary to complete the project. Team members should be braced to provide information about their work on the project and their perceived levels of effort. They should have some familiarity with how they have done this work in the past and a clear vision of what the ultimate outcome of this project is to be.

Bottom-up task-oriented WBS construction is an idea-generation activity and can use some of the most familiar idea-generation techniques. Brainstorming, the Crawford Slip, Nominal Group Technique, and other idea-generation tools can be used to generate a broad ranging (albeit incomplete) list of activities. You can get additional insights on these techniques in Appendix A—Idea-Generation Techniques for Designing an Effective WBS. The project manager's first mission in this type of WBS construction is to get as many activities associated with the project identified as possible. This hodgepodge of activities will serve as the foundation from which the team will work to build a more conventional WBS.

Once team members have identified as many work packages as they can, the project manager should organize these within the company's life-cycle approach. If there is no standard life-cycle approach, the old convention of Concept, Development, Implementation, and Termination can readily be applied. (For example, the project manager would ask team members, "Is this a Development or Implementation activity?") By getting the team members to agree on where these activities should belong, the project manager not only works toward WBS completion but also generates a clearer sense of the network or time-oriented relationships among the activities.

One tool that is extremely effective for manipulating this information is the use of yellow sticky notes or Post-Its®. Activities documented on Post-Its can then be easily maneuvered from one phase to another in the discussion.

Once all the information is grouped according to its proper phase, the project manager and team members can begin to identify information gaps. Initially, this is relatively easy, as overlapping activities are eliminated and obvious holes are quickly filled. Sometimes, however, the voids are more subtle and require more extensive attention and remediation.

Bottom-Up Task-Oriented WBS Checklist

1. Have you identified all the deliverables associated with this project? Have they been mapped to a contract compliance matrix or other document outlining all of the deliverables? Insert these at the work package level of the WBS.

Success Criteria: All of the deliverables have been defined and mapped in the contract, requirements document, statement of work, and other documentation. Organizational and administrative support requirements are included.

2. Have you grouped the tasks into logical summaries, keeping the groupings to less than several dozen activities per summary? Have they been assigned at the cost account level (one level above the work package)?

Success Criteria: All of the work packages have been grouped under logical summaries at the cost account level. No cost account captures more than several dozen activities. Each cost account has at least two work packages under it.

3. Have you grouped the cost accounts into logical summaries, keeping the groupings to less than several dozen cost accounts?

Success Criteria: All of the cost accounts have been grouped under logical summaries at the next level up the WBS. No summary captures more than several dozen cost accounts. Each summary has at least two cost accounts under it.

4. Have you grouped the summaries into higher summaries (or to the project level), keeping the groupings to less than several dozen summaries?

Success Criteria: All of the summaries have been grouped under higher-level logical summaries at the next level up the WBS. No higher-level summary captures more than several dozen lower-level summaries. Each higher-level summary has at least two lower-level summaries under it.

5. Have you repeated step #4 enough to gather the summaries up to the project level?

Success Criteria: All of the highest-level summaries (often phases or key components) have been identified and grouped under the name of the project at the top of the WBS.

6. Have you gone back through the project and assigned numerical values to the project, the summaries, the cost accounts, and the work packages?

Success Criteria: Each element of the WBS has a numerical value assigned which identifies its relative position within the structure.

Filling the Gaps

The greatest challenge in filling the voids within a work breakdown structure is discovering what work has to be done (that's either never been done before or is unfamiliar to the organization). Toward that end, project managers can use a variety of approaches:

- Networking
- Delphi Technique
- Consultant Validation
- Template Comparison

Each technique has its merits and its limitations. Project managers creating a WBS need to recognize that, first and foremost, the WBS is a living, breathing document. To assume that a WBS will survive the project without change is to assume that every project parameter, from requirements to resources to risks, will remain constant. It is a risky and unrealistic assumption.

Networking

The networking approach is potentially the most thorough and exhaustive of the bottom-up WBS gap removal techniques. It is also potentially time-consuming and draining for the project manager and team members alike. Before embarking on the networking approach, the project manager should review the networking applicability checklist to see if it is appropriate in their environment. The process involves identifying all of the inputs and all of the outputs for each activity in the WBS *and* where those inputs come from (and where the outputs go).

Networking Applicability Checklist

- Does the project require numerous activities in serial?

- Can all of the key functional members be present for the WBS development session?

- Are team members familiar with the project deliverables and the organization's processes and practices?

- Are team members willing to offer their perspectives on the best sequencing of activities?

- Can team members (or their managers) commit to sequences based on the outcome of the session?

- Is the organization willing to consider and/or accept approaches other than the conventional ones?

- Will team members be able to reason through the activities and deliverables required for them to achieve their tasks?

The Networking approach is best done with the responsible team members present. It has the potential to generate intense sentiments in terms of what can and should be accomplished and how the work should be done. Project managers should alert team members to the potential conflicts *before* the effort begins, so that everyone can acknowledge that the intensity of the discussion is normal and can be productive if it focuses on systems and processes, rather than on personalities.

To work through the networking approach, the project manager can use either of two approaches. The first is to create subgroups and to allow these groups to network their own small portions of the project plan for later integration into the final plan. The second is to work through the entire process with the entire team. The former approach is best when there are more than 10 team members involved. Rarely can 10 people working as a group all make significant contributions to the outcome. In smaller teams, the entire group can work together, thus avoiding the later integration step. By dropping that step, the team can save significant time and energy.

In either approach, team members take each activity and ask the simple questions:

- What inputs are required to get this activity underway?

- What deliverables will this activity produce?

The first question should drive the team toward the beginning of the project, working forward until all of the activities have been identified. If an input is not available either in stock in the organization or as an output of another activity, another step should be added to the WBS. Thus, a gap is identified, and the hole in the plan is filled.

The second question drives the team toward the end of the project. Team members should work back from the end of the project by first asking if the deliverable goes directly to the customer. If it does not, then the successor activity must exist elsewhere in the WBS. If there is no successor activity to take advantage of the deliverable produced, either the work is superfluous or another gap is identified and another activity is added to the WBS.

The work here is painstaking. It is frustrating and, in a WBS of several hundred activities, will take the better part of a day. The rewards, however, are numerous. The project manager who completes this process has the full team's perspective on what steps need to be done and (as a bonus) the sequence in which those steps should be performed. While the WBS is not a scheduling tool, its role as support for the schedule is clearly evident in this environment.

The other major advantage here is that team members have the opportunity to discuss and challenge different approaches to the work and to engage in a healthy debate on the most effective ways to accommodate the customer's needs. Team effort and a concerted approach to the project plan result.

Beyond the time-consuming nature of the work, the other critical issue with this type of WBS generation is validation. The best oarsmen, no matter how good, do not add speed to a powerboat. A team without critical skills and capabilities will be of little assistance to the project manager in crafting a quality project plan.

This approach allows team members to proffer ideas that they may not have previously shared and to outline tactics and strategies that were unacceptable or were not examined before. It also affords the project manager an opportunity to build new templates and new methodologies for dealing with old, as well as new, problems.

Once the approach is complete, the project manager should still take steps to ensure the project plan is validated by professionals, accepted within the organization and, at a more critical/significant level, reviewed and understood by the customer. In many instances, this can be accomplished by simply working with the other parties involved (customer, subcontractors, functional support managers) to see if they concur with the approach. A word of warning, however—reviewers will invariably have suggestions. How the project manager deals with them at this point will dictate the team's position on issues relating to these suggestions. Choose reviewers carefully.

The best reviewers are those who have been involved in work of a similar nature and who will respect the project manager's final decision. They may include peer project managers, functional managers who support the project, or lower-echelon executives. They should understand their role as reviewers (not project managers) and work effectively within that role. In proposal development, they parallel the "white team" that does a friendly, supportive review identifying potential improvements. They should not assume the role of the "red team" that does an adversarial review on every aspect of the current plan.

Upon completion of the review, the project manager may be ready to finalize and document the WBS. The project manager may choose to apply one of the other gap analysis tools to complete the effort. The project manager can assess the success of the network analysis approach using the following checklist.

Networking Approach Checklist

1. Are all of the deliverables outlined in the contract produced by the WBS?

Success Criteria: In a compliance matrix of contract deliverables, activities can be identified within the WBS which produce each deliverable required under the contract.

2. Does the WBS support all organizational processes?

Success Criteria: Organizational documentation requirements are met by the WBS and the approach to the work is in keeping with organizational mandate and capability,

3. Do team members concur that the approach will work?

Success Criteria: Team members acknowledge that the work, as identified, will lead to the completion of all deliverables required under the contract. *(Note: Team members do not have to choose the same approach; only acknowledge that the approach chosen is achievable.)*

4. Do team members and functional managers concur that the approach is an effective use of resources?

Success Criteria: Functional management signs off on the associated documentation, including the Project Charter authorizing resource use.

5. Have team members signed off on the finished WBS?

Success Criteria: Team members sign the WBS, an accompanying memorandum, or other documentation that acknowledges their role in its creation and their acceptance of the final document.

Delphi Technique

The Delphi Technique is named, appropriately enough, for the Oracle at Delphi. Greek mythology tells that Delphi was sacred to the god Apollo. In the temple of Apollo at Delphi, ancient Greeks would ask questions of a woman (Pythia) who was believed to communicate the knowledge of the gods (although she would utter weird sounds as she flailed wildly through the temple). The priests would then interpret what Apollo was saying through this woman. Unlike the wild behavior exhibited by Pythia, the Delphi Technique as applied to modern-day project management requires that project managers draw on their own experts' knowledge of the organization.

The process normally involves a panel of experts usually based outside an office. In this instance, the WBS (or the appropriate sections of the WBS) would be forwarded to the experts for their individual review and comment.

As a review cycle draws to a close, the project manager collects the comments, generates an updated version of the work breakdown structure, and forwards the updated version *back* to the experts.

The experts then review the updated version; offer their additions, deletions, or corrections; and return the WBS to the project manager. The cycle continues until the project manager is satisfied with the outcome, and the WBS is deemed complete by all concerned.

The advantage of the Delphi Technique is that the project manager gets to draw on the expertise of some of the organization's most knowledgeable personnel within a reasonable period of time. The key disadvantage of the Delphi Technique is the inordinate amount of time required to complete the process. Even two or three cycles through the process can consume weeks, as project managers wait for the experts to return their opinions. Even the best-intentioned experts may miss deadlines and subvert the goals of the thorough WBS analysis.

The advent of e-mail, Internet newsgroups, and some specific concept analysis software applications can significantly reduce the time involved in the Delphi Technique, but the approach ultimately relies on the timely responses of experts. The relationship between the project manager and the experts will often determine whether the approach succeeds or fails.

Project managers can determine early if they'll be successful in using the Delphi Technique. A review of the checklist can help determine whether it is the best approach.

Delphi Technique Applicability Checklist

1. Are there subject matter experts within the organization?

2. Are they unavailable for direct contribution in a group session?

3. Is there time available for give and take via e-mail or conventional mail?

4. Is the project manager skilled at distilling information and presenting it clearly?

5.   Are there potentially different approaches (with similar levels of validity) to achieve the same results?

If the project team decides on the Delphi Technique, the project manager must take the lead role in terms of collecting and disseminating information. Applied appropriately, the technique results in the collection of inputs that reflect only the best elements from the experts.

The project manager should also be aware of the "politics" that may arise in using this technique. In some organizations, "experts" may actually expect their input to be used. They may assert their influence to force management to reconsider the WBS and the approaches in use. The Delphi Technique, while an excellent means for validating a Bottom-up WBS, has potential political drawbacks the project manager must be aware of.

Consultant Validation

Many organizations consider themselves incapable of assessing the Work Breakdown Structure. While they deem themselves the "experts" in accomplishing the project, they doubt their own capacity to break the work down into logical subcomponents that are assignable and for which accountability can be expected. In some instances, they hire consultants to identify gaps in the WBS.

The challenge associated with consultant validation is, frankly, validating the consultant. It's relatively easy to find consultants to do the work. The difficulty lies in finding consultants who are familiar with the approaches that an organization uses in performing such projects.

Finding a consultant who can live up to the pressures and demands of an organization may hinge on the consultant's understanding of the organization, its bureaucracy, and its internal idiosyncrasies. Bringing in outside help may sometimes consume as much time and energy as creating the WBS inhouse.

Consultants have the potential to make significant contributions if they can meet the criteria cited below.

Consultant Validation Applicability Checklist

1. Is the consultant aware of organizational practice, policy, and idiosyncrasies?

Success Criteria: The consultant has worked for the organization before, has researched the organization extensively, or is prepared to do a fundamental organizational review before beginning work.

2. Is the consultant aware of the needs of the customer?

Success Criteria: The consultant has worked for the customer before, has researched the organization, has reviewed the contract, and/or has worked extensively for the customer's direct competition.

3. Does the consultant know and understand the work to be performed?

Success Criteria: The consultant has done work of a similar nature, or has consulted on similar projects.

4. Is the consultant familiar with the organization's approach in building WBSs?

Success Criteria: The consultant concurs with the organization's approach to WBS construction, and has developed similar WBS in the past on projects of a similar scope.

With consultant validation, it's most effective to use consultants who have worked with the organization and who know what is acceptable and what is not. Failure to recognize the limitations of outside consultants can lead to a situation where the project is hampered by unnecessary or redundant activities.

Template Comparison

Another technique for evaluating the bottom-up approach to WBS construction is template comparison. While templates will be discussed in depth later in this document, it is important to acknowledge their role here as a tool for evaluating and creating a WBS.

It is not the objective of this technique to create a mirror image of a past one. Instead, the template is used to examine experiences and conventional approaches used in past projects. Templates generally reflect the lessons learned and represent a crucial source of information and experience.

A template comparison is not a one-for-one review. What a template can provide, however, is a perspective on the critical issues, deliverables, or phases that have been essential to past successes. With that information, it becomes possible to evaluate whether or not the current WBS has the potential to achieve a similar level of success.

To conduct a template comparison, the template must be dissected to identify the critical components. It will be most valuable at the highest levels and progressively less valuable as you work down into the minutiae. For each summary level of the template, there should be either a corresponding level in WBS or a rationalization as to why that level is not essential to the project. The rationalizations explain why certain approaches were used and why certain approaches were dropped. While the comparison may yield little change in the newly generated WBS, it often serves to provide affirmation that the new bottom-up approach makes the most sense.

Once again, it's important to understand that template comparison of a bottom-up WBS is not the same as the generation of a new WBS from a template, which will be discussed shortly.

As with the other types of work breakdown structure, a checklist is provided here to ensure the work has been done properly.

Template Construction

Many project managers tend to refer to older projects and the WBS that were used before when constructing new ones. This is a favorite approach in organizations where project management methodologies build a certain level of consistency in the project environment.

Even though the objective of templates is to encourage effective repetition of quality work, it's important to ensure that they're used properly. The tragedy with some project management methodologies is that they tend to serve and conform to the organization's policies rather than serve the customer's needs.

To avoid this, the project manager needs to work through a series of steps ensuring that the template has been modified to meet the customer's needs, to address current organizational reality, and to reflect current technical practice.

Meeting the Customer's Needs

To meet the customer's needs, the project manager should turn to the statement of work, project requirements document, contract, internal work order, or other documentation generated to identify all the activities needed to complete the project. (Only then can the project manager get the template appropriate to the work.)

Some organizations have "one-size-fits-all" templates for all projects. Such templates primarily address organizational and administrative issues, rather than specific customer concerns. If they claim to address customer issues as well, the manager must make sure that the templates are sufficiently flexible to resolve conflicts with customization, specific customer needs, and the vagaries of different contracts. (In actual situations, templates are flexible).

Other organizations have a variety of "cookie-cutter" templates to deal with their "standard" projects. Customers request a particular deliverable, and the organization applies the template used to produce that deliverable. This is one step more advanced than a "one-size-fits-all" approach but still has significant drawbacks in terms of direct, customized service.

Still other organizations use templates of past projects that are provided from other organizations or from software packages. These have merit, but it's important to recognize their limitations.

A model established by the software industry in prototyping involves leaving what software programmers refer to as "stubs" in their code. In prototyping, the general framework for software is established, but much of the functionality is left out for the sake of avoiding extensive rework and rebuilding. In constructing a WBS using a template, much the same approach can be used.

Specifically, the best templates will be those that provide the organizational framework for doing the work but which leave "stubs" where customer-specific information can be plugged in. Such an approach allows the project manager to incorporate all of the lessons learned from past projects and, at the same time, opens the door to innovation and creativity in crafting a customer solution.

Those who argue that standardized templates for standardized work are sufficient tend to work from the premise that projects are truly repeatable. This is counter to the standard, accepted definition of projects as unique, time-limited, budget-constrained, customer-driven experiences.

Templates are borne out of organizational experience. Quality templates incorporate the vast experiences of the organization, its project managers, and the customers themselves. Consulting organizations will sometimes claim they have the capacity to build WBS templates as part of an organization's project management methodology. Unless they draw on organizational experience in constructing it, such claim should be suspect.

The key question for the project manager considering template use should be whether or not the template will actually cover all of the information it must cover in order to be effective. A quality template should provide insight on the work to be accomplished, the processes for reporting that work, and the organizational environment in which the work must be conducted.

The work is broken up into two categories. There are organizational mandates (practices and processes which are standard to your organization) and customer-specific work. Standardizing the WBS in a template (even down to the work package level) for organizational mandates is plausible. Organizations have specific "boilerplate" steps that they expect will be taken with each project, each time. They don't expect the process to change, and they expect project managers to carry it out as part of their duties. These components are relatively easy to standardize in a WBS template. For customer-specific work, however, the standardization is far more challenging. If an organization works from multiple templates, there may be a template available to deliver a particular product or service. If so, the level of detail on these components may be driven down as far as the cost account (reporting level), and rarely, the work package. It is still prudent to allow the Project manager to identify the specific tasks that will be performed, as customer demands (including reporting, staffing, and scheduling) may drive modifications at the work package level.

In an environment where multiple WBS templates are available, the "stubs" discussed earlier will appear at the cost account level, just one level above the work package. The general processes will be outlined in sufficient depth that only the customer-specific work packages need to be added.

Even though WBS templates (theoretically) represent the best practice and best thinking of an organization, they should be considered living, breathing documents. The WBS should never be perceived as static. Just as technologies, customer approaches, and internal processes change, the WBS must change over time. At the end of each project, Project managers should take responsibility for identifying which elements of the template served them well, which were dispensable, and which were missing altogether.

If an organization works from a "one-size-fits-all" model, the project manager needs additional information tracking steps to fill the gaps. Some project manager s achieve this by creating a supplemental level below the formal work package level of the standardized WBS. By doing so, they have sufficient flexibility to document and track customer concerns. While it is not "best practice" to augment organizational mandates, it is essential that all of the work, even that which does not fit into the organizational model, be identified and addressed in the work breakdown structure.

Organizations do not always invest the time and energy required to build templates for each type of project and to track their relative levels of success. In such cases, project managers may use project management software packages which come equipped with a plethora of templates that they can adapt to their work environment.

Microsoft Project 98, for example, came equipped with the following templates:

- Aerospace
- Event Planning
- Intranet
- ISO 9000
- Renovation
- Software Launch

In the original DOS version of *Timeline,* the software came equipped with templates ranging from basic construction to the grand opening of a zoo. While few project managers will ever be called upon to manage a zoo opening, such templates can readily be adapted to accommodate other types of grand openings.

The key is to recognize that these baseline "model" projects were not built in a specific organizational environment.   Instead, they were built by professionals to emulate what project managers *might* experience in the field. Thus, even *Timeline*'s old zoo template wouldn't necessarily be a one-for-one match with every zoo-opening project. These templates provide a foundation of information, but they should not be considered complete. They are complete only when they have been thoroughly reviewed for their applicability.

In some organizations, the only concern with the WBS template is the process for reporting the work. These WBS frameworks are basic outlines that require additional tailoring. It is valuable as long as the project manager recognizes its limitations. The template is not intended to outline the project effort in any way, shape, or form.

A sample template follows:

1.0 System (This should provide a 2-to-5-word description of the system to be delivered. Reporting at this level is provided to the Board of Directors.)

   1.1 Subsystem (This should identify a key component of the system. No more than seven subsystems should be identified at this level. In the XYZ Corporation, this serves to identify subsystems produced by the various functional organizations. Reporting at this level is provided to the President.)

      1.1.1 Subcomponents (This should identify subcomponents of the system. No more than 10 subcomponents should be identified at this level for any given subsystem. In the XYZ Corporation, this level identifies the key elements of the deliverable to be produced. Reporting at this level is provided to the Program Manager.)

1.1.1.1   Cost Account (This should identify key elements of the subcomponents of the system. No more than 14 cost accounts should be identified at this level for any given subcomponent. In the XYZ Corporation, this level identifies the parts or hardware or deliverables required to produce a given subcomponent. Reporting at this level is provided to the functional managers on their resources only).

1.1.1.1.1   Work Package (This should identify, in verb-object format, the activity required to produce the cost account. This is where hours of effort will be assigned. Information at this level will be networked into a critical path schedule. In the XYZ Corporation, this level is where tasks are compared to a contract compliance matrix. Reporting at this level is for the project manager 's use).

Without listing *any* project specifics, this template provides project managers critical information at each level. By identifying the reporting levels, it gives the project manager a better handle on what activities should be included for that level. "Is this something the Program Manager needs visibility on?" The outline provides a measure of consistency as they develop effective work breakdown structures.

In small projects, however, project manager s will have difficulty generating enough information to fill a WBS down to the fifth level. One solution is to have only one or two activities in the first two or three levels of the WBS. A fundamental rule of WBS construction specifies breaking a parent activity into at least two sub-activities.

Some WBS templates also attempt to reflect the organizational environment. In many instances, these templates provide guidance on the supporting information *surrounding* the WBS—not guidance on the information that goes *into* the WBS.

Rather than breaking down the WBS level by level, this type of template identifies what supporting information the project manager or the project team needs. Often, the project manager will record this information in a project management software, such as *M/S Project* or *ABT Project Workbench*. This is the information that is presented in the spreadsheet view, horizontally, out from the activity name. It may include everything from duration, resource name, risk assignments, fixed cost, to organizational reports. It does *not* provide supplemental guidance on how to build the WBS—only on what information the organization requires.

The checklist below identifies some of the key questions the project manager should ask in order to determine if a particular template will serve the organization's needs.

Template Checklist

1. Is the template designed only to provide structure—not content—for the WBS?

Success criteria: Templates designed to provide structure and level guidance are inherently appropriate and need not be reviewed further. Templates designed to provide guidance on content should be reviewed using the rest of this checklist.

2. If the template is designed to provide content, is the content appropriate to this project?

Success criteria: Templates in which all activities in the template mirror the activities that must be performed for this customer and for this deliverable need not be reviewed further. Templates in which the content needs modification should be reviewed further.

3. If the template has been built using "stubs" (undefined cost accounts), do the stubs provide a framework under which the work packages for this particular customer can be built?

Success criteria: The cost account level of the WBS effectively summarizes the specific work to be done at the work package level.

4. If the template uses a generic project (either internal or via a popular software package), can the project be modified reasonably to adapt to the current customer's deliverables and expectations?

Success criteria: The generic project is at least tangentially related to the current effort and will not require a rewrite of more than 50% of the activities.

5. Once the template has been established, has it been modified to effectively deal with the needs of this particular effort?

Success criteria: All of the work packages have been grouped under logical summaries at the cost account level. Each cost account has at least two work packages under it. The work packages map to a compliance matrix of the customer's demands.

6. Do all the parties involved recognize the WBS as a viable means for accomplishing the work?

Success criteria: The customer signs off on the WBS (at a high level) and the project team signs off on the WBS (at a detailed level).

Hybrids

As with any business practice, there will always be hybrid approaches—that is, a combination of one or two methods. Some project managers will use a template only up to a point and then convert to a bottom-up networked approach. Others will start with their own internal projects and modify them based on information provided in a template. As we mentioned earlier, there are very few hard and fast rules relating to the WBS. The work breakdown structure is a tool that project managers must design based on their organizations' resources and their customers' needs. To claim that there is only one way to do it is to be inflexible and impractical.

As with all of the approaches, the determination of whether or not a hybrid is appropriate stems from the organization, the type of project and the project manager involved, and the customers' needs. If there are organizational mandates to use a particular type of WBS, a hybrid may be the most flexible approach to accommodate the restrictions imposed by these mandates.

The Living, Growing WBS

Any respected literature on work breakdown structure construction emphasizes that it is a living, constantly changing document. It flexes with the project, growing and changing as the project environment changes. The project manager must ensure that WBS changes are recorded effectively and communicated regularly to the team. It is also important to ensure that the WBS, in its original form, is preserved for historical reference and to identify "best practice" for future projects of a similar nature.

Recording the WBS in both its original and iterative forms is not as administratively challenging as it might seem. In reality, the project manager need only use one current project management software package to track the original version, as well as the iterations. Most of the current tools allow for the original (baseline) WBS and as many as nine interim versions. We need that information to provide reports to the team, to the customer, and to management as to why the project changed, how it changed, and the relative impact of the change on the project activity hierarchy.

In making the changes, it's vital to recognize one key trait of the WBS. It is a hierarchy of the work to be performed and the subsets of that work. It is *not* a schedule. That means when the project manager adds activities to the WBS, they are added as a component of the work, not as components of the schedule. Consider the following section of a baseline WBS for painting an auditorium:

    1.1.2   Paint Preparation

        1.1.2.1   Scrub Walls
        1.1.2.2   Mask Windows
        1.1.2.3   Mask Trim
        1.1.2.4   Sand Walls
        1.1.2.5   Scrub Walls (second time)

As the project team begins work on this effort, they discover numerous pits, cracks, and nicks in the walls. They determine that some putty will have to be applied in certain spots to ensure a smooth surface. The project manager must add an activity titled "Apply putty to damaged areas." The other activities were already established in chronological order, so there is a temptation to insert that activity in chronological fashion (somewhere between 1.1.2.1 and 1.1.2.4).

However, in projects where there are dozens of activities under a given summary, such an insertion could lead to confusion among other team members whose activities may be affected. Ideally, when activities are added, they should be added within the correct summary, but as the last activity under that summary. Thus, "Apply Putty to Damaged Areas" would become activity 1.1.2.6 in the WBS.

With a Gantt (horizontal bar) chart, for example, practitioners tend to view the WBS as "correct" when it is organized in a tidy stair-step fashion.

This impression, is misleading and simplistic. When task numbers constantly change, there is greater potential for miscommunication and confusion in the assignment of personnel and material resources.

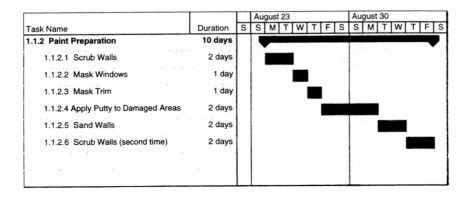

Properly modified, the amended WBS will look more like this:

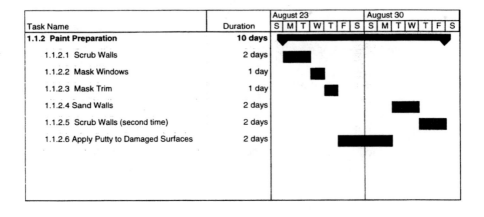

With this WBS, it will be easier to track the information, to assign resources, to get accurate reports, to ensure that the history of the WBS' development is accurately preserved and, most important, to periodically add new work packages.

New activities should be added to the WBS as soon as they are identified. As with the earlier example, they should be incorporated at the bottom of the summary group. As various iterations of the WBS are tracked, the project manager determines what activities were added and how the organization's processes were affected.

Adding activities is not the only change that can happen in a WBS. The same fundamental rules should apply as activities are deleted. The project history is far more effectively tracked if the project manager lives with the absence of one number in the sequence.

The project manager should also recognize that some additions and adjustments to the WBS are made in an *ad hoc* fashion. Team members often recognize minor shortcomings in the project plan and take additional activities or steps to complete the work. Some project managers see no need to record these activities in the WBS because they were completed and they did not affect the overall schedule and cost. It is, after all, a planning document. They see the WBS merely as a planning tool for the current project and fail to recognize its role and contributions to future ones.

In organizations that apply methodologies or templates, there may be a temptation to forego these types of WBS modifications. Project managers may feel that their only responsibility is to live up to the requirements of the WBS as prescribed by the organization. This view is constricting in that it does not explore better ways to accomplish the work within the customers' environment. Organizations that hope to grow in project management should gather these modifications and use them to work toward improved work breakdown structures for future projects.

Chapter 3

Communicating WBS Changes

In addition to recording the changes properly, the project manager must communicate changes to the WBS to the team, in general, and the responsible parties, in particular. Communicating this information can be extraordinarily complex in projects where the WBS covers activities that span not only long periods of time, but vast distances as well. For each change, the project manager needs to know which team members to notify and when they need to be alerted.

The change notification methodology will vary from project to project and even from team member to team member. Invariably, some nuances of the project will drive the project manager to try different tactics in sharing vital project information.

Some of the most basic project management change information is communicated through the WBS itself. In some organizations, the WBS is maintained in a central location, with broad access via a local area network (LAN) or wide area network (WAN). In either case, just because the WBS is widely available does *not* ensure that it will be widely accessed. Many team members feel that they either already know the work that's being done or that they will receive some alternative form of notification if there is a significant change in the work. They seldom review updated WBS for changes.

In such an environment, project managers should regularly e-mail changes to the team members. Many of the newer project management software packages have e-mail links that allow for easy communication with the project team whenever their work packages are modified. However, these links normally notify only those team members who are directly impacted by the change—that is, they normally notify only those team members who are assigned to the activities. Knowing this, it's important to acknowledge the owners of other activities under the same summary activity because, while their activity may not change, their expectations may change significantly based on the outputs of the other work being performed.

In the painting project cited earlier, the addition of the putty work may directly affect only those responsible for applying the putty. It may, however, indirectly affect those doing the sanding, the painting, and the trim. This modest change needs to be communicated across the organization.

In a LAN or WAN environment, using the local software version of the project plan and e-mail notification may be adequate. In large-scale projects with geographically distributed teams, more work is involved. The information communication need remains the same. The owner of the affected activity and the owners of related activities need to know about the change. The challenge here is sharing the information without inundating the project team with too much data. Too many "change alerts" can be just as damaging (if not more so) as too few. Team members who receive virtually daily notice of changes will, over time, grow numb to the information, eventually missing critical data.

This is particularly a concern in an environment where geographical dispersion makes regular team meetings and ready LAN/WAN access more challenging. The Internet provides one alternative, as most project management tools allow for hypertext markup language (HTML) "saves" of critical project information, while some of the more advanced tools allow for Internet reporting and tracking. By using the Internet tools, the project manager can provide information in familiar formats, and do so via popular and constantly used access.

The project manager must emphasize to the team members the importance of regularly reviewing the changes to the WBS. The project manager needs to let the team know the consequences if they miss a change or if they pursue an approach that's been abandoned. Project lessons learned files are littered with the tales of project team members who wasted valuable time on approaches that had been shelved.

Some project managers use the WBS as a repository for interesting project notes, histories, and episodes. One PM in an ESI International classroom mentioned that she occasionally incorporated references to personal anecdotes ("war stories") in the "Notes" field of the software package, and posted the notes on the Web as a sort of Project Newsletter for team members to read. The personal anecdotes became a resource of both insight and project humor for the various parties involved. More important, she also included information about upcoming modifications to the WBS. By keeping the site refreshed and updated, she *encouraged* team members to visit it where, in the process, they picked up critical information and gained a better understanding of both their activities and the project as a whole.

Project managers handling larger endeavors use newsletters to provide information about changes in the WBS. Such newsletters can be very effective if they consistently provide valuable information. Like a quality newspaper, a newsletter can be judged by its ability to report the latest events in a timely, comprehensive fashion.

Other project managers will prefer to communicate project changes personally. This is perhaps the single most popular approach to providing information about the project. The great challenge here is twofold. First, the project manager must ensure that the information is provided regularly. Second, the project manager must ensure that the information is properly recorded. Providing information on a consistent basis sounds simple enough. In reality, though, it is difficult to achieve.

Project managers communicate effectively with some team members and less effectively with others. On a similar note, some team members easily embrace change; others are challenged by it. Whatever the case is, the project manager can overcome these concerns by documenting all the information—"change talking points"—by inserting these points into the "Notes" field of the project management software as they are discussed and as the WBS is modified.

This step brings us to another critical issue—that of version control. As the team implements changes, the WBS must change. But the operative question is "Which WBS?" In many projects, team members access a centralized copy and maintain their own copies of a WBS. With geographically dispersed project teams, this may result in several "master copies" of the work breakdown structure. As the project team documents change, there will be different versions of the plan with varying levels of information.

This poses a problem for the project manager who needs to determine what work has been accomplished, what work has been paid for, what work is billable, and what work had to be modified to meet the customers' needs. The need to centralize and control these changes then becomes imperative.

There are several solutions. A good example is the Internet. By using some of the Internet-based tools, a single master HTML version of the WBS can be maintained in a central repository on a Web server, with varying levels of access for the project manager and other team members. This approach works well in limiting the access of team members (in terms of their ability to change areas outside their purview) and in granting them access to the tools. It does, however, require some education on the tools for those who are not Internet-savvy.

Without Internet capabilities, the project manager may consider "group updates" to the WBS. In such an environment, the project manager brings together the multiple copies of the WBS from the various sites for a concurrence update. Any disparities are documented, and all of the small changes that have been made are assimilated into a single, master document. The project manager then sends out the new master WBS to all of the locations until the next group update is conducted.

In both environments, one question persists. Who is responsible for change to the WBS? Who has the authority to make the changes? In an ideal universe, the WBS would not have to change. Reality is seldom ideal. In the field, the project manager must determine who can make changes and with what levels of frequency and notification. While this is a component of a much larger subject of control, for this monograph, we will limit discussion to controlling change on the WBS.

The very nature of projects propels the people involved in them—customers, team members, functional managers, and project managers—to continually undertake new activities and approaches even after they have established the project baseline. Such a situation creates problems—in communication, accountability, version control, among other things. It is important that project stakeholders agree on how and when the WBS is changed. Specifically, they must agree on how WBS version control will be managed from the start.

Some project managers become *so* controlling that they refuse to allow anyone else to see, work with, modify, or review the WBS. It is important for team members to access the latest iteration of the WBS so they can effectively perform their work.

The checklist will help you decide on the most effective version control method to use.

Version Control Checklist

1. Have we established an approach that will facilitate change to the WBS?

Success criteria: The approach allows for change to the project plan as change is authorized. The approach mirrors the capabilities of the change control system in place for the project.

2. Do team members know how the process works?

Success criteria: Team members who know the processes involved can either input changes to the WBS or forward such changes to the WBS authority for documentation.

3. Does the process ensure consistency in the WBS?

Success criteria: Multiple versions of the WBS are made available to team members as they are regularly updated to reflect the changes made in other iterations. The frequency of the updates is determined by the project duration—short projects need more frequent updates, while multi-year projects need longer intervals.

4. Using the process, does the WBS reflect all the work to be done?

Success criteria: All activities and team member time critical to the project are reflected and can be accounted for within the WBS.

5. Does the process still grant access?

Success criteria: The control processes in place are flexible enough that team members can readily access and review the WBS for updates.

6. Upon project completion, does the WBS reflect the "as-built" condition of the project?

Success criteria: Particularly in a configuration management environment, there is traceability between the project, the specifications, and the WBS. In other management environment, the WBS accurately reflects all components of the deliverable (or tasks performed) and all work required to bring those components together.

Chapter 4

Closing Out the WBS

The Project Management Institute stresses that, at the end of the project, the WBS should reflect the "as-built" condition of that project. With the advent of numerous project management methodologies, some project managers prefer to push in the opposite direction. There's a temptation to build the WBS to reflect the "as-built" condition of the organization's methodology, rather than the as-built condition of the project. That's wrong.

It's vital to reflect all of the work that's been done and all of the components of the project after the work is completed (not just as it was planned). If the project manager fails to accurately track the information, the organization will lose a lot of lessons learned from the project and won't be able to accurately replicate the work that was done well.

In order to ensure the WBS is closed out properly, open WBS activities must be reviewed. If they were actually closed (but forgotten), the project manager should track down the team members responsible and ask them how long it took to complete the work and whether or not they encountered any problems with the work.

Organizations often fail to recognize the value of small tasks that team members took without authorization or without formal documentation in the WBS. Toward that end, project managers need to conduct exit interviews with the team members to ensure that all tasks are accurately documented. The form below serves as a template that you can modify and use in the exit interview.

Exit Interview Form			
Project Name	Team Member		
Functional Area	Date of Exit Interview		
1	Were there any general "Lessons Learned" associated with this project?		
2	Please label each activity you were assigned to as either completed or incomplete. If the task is incomplete, please give a brief explanation.		
Task Number:			
Task Number:			
Task Number:			
Task Number:			
Task Number:			
Task Number:			
3	Many projects require additional, *ad hoc* activities that weren't part of the project plan. Were any such activities required in your area? If so, please provide a brief description of the task, resources, and duration.		
	Description	Duration	Resources
A			
B			
C			
D			
E			
4	If the organization decides to do a similar project in the future, what general suggestions would you offer to the next team or project manager to improve performance?		

By completing an exit interview form, the team member provides (1) insights on how the organization can enhance its ability to do projects in the future and (2) guidance to current projects. This is important because many organizations fail to realize that they can eliminate recurring mistakes by simply changing their approach.

In addition to tasks, the project manager must ensure that all of the project deliverables are reflected in the final WBS. Particularly in deliverables-oriented WBS, the project manager must ensure that all of the deliverables to the customer are completely documented in the WBS for future reference. Every activity should be directly linked to a deliverable in this structure and, thus, every deliverable should be traceable back into the WBS. An activity should be created and documented for deliverables not linked to the WBS to complete the documentation.

Storage and Retrieval

At the completion of a project, a WBS that was created and nurtured as its foundation and framework usually ends up in the forgotten file. Such an ignominious fate should not befall the WBS. A WBS should be preserved, analyzed, and reviewed to ensure that the lessons learned can be applied time and time again as the organization evolves in project management. Every WBS should be seen as another brick in the pathway that leads to project management excellence.

To do this, the WBS must be stored in a central repository. After the final reviews, the WBS should be stored in a location where project managers from across the organization can access it. If it's stored electronically, it should be preserved in a "read-only" format to ensure that it is not modified by others who may wish to use it as a template for future efforts. If they're trying to create a template, they can save it under a different name on their own system, rather than modify organizational history.

Ideally, these documents should be preserved with keywords that highlight their primary achievements. If a particular WBS served well in a service project with ISO 9000 for the Widget Corporation, it will be easier to find under "ISO" than under "Widget" for those unfamiliar with clients and their individual projects. Thus, cross-referencing and search keywords become crucial. Project managers should be compelled to identify a minimum of eight keywords associated with their WBS. Those keywords may include:

- Customer name
- Project name
- Key deliverable(s)
- Lead customer contact
- Lead organizational contact
- Critical learning
- Patent numbers
- Project type
- Functional organization
- Executive sponsor
- Awards won
- Resources
- Nicknames (yes, even projects get nicknames)

By encouraging project managers to file the projects under these keywords, the valuable lessons learned of past work breakdown structures will not be lost to other PMs in the future.

In cataloging the WBS, it is best is to preserve the most current version with clear identification of those tasks that were dropped, forgotten, *or* added along the way. If that's not possible, or if the WBS is not being preserved in a digital format, save only the baseline and the final version, unless there is historic significance to the other iterations. Saving too many versions of the WBS leads to confusion and may almost be as bad as not saving any version at all.

On a final note, make sure the project managers' telephone numbers and last known location are recorded with the WBS, because there will always be questions down the road. An effective and vigilant project manager works to continually share insight and lessons learned so that the organization can formulate better work breakdown structures.

Idea-Generation Techniques
For Designing
An Effective WBS

Brainstorming

The process of brainstorming is simple. The project manager begins by clearly identifying the objective of the project. This objective should be expressed in as much detail as possible so it is clear to all team members. It's also a good idea to identify the orientation of the work breakdown structure (task-oriented or product-oriented) for later categorization. If the orientation is already known, the highest levels of the WBS should be visually displayed to guide team members during discussion.

In a brainstorm, the ideas of all team members are catalogued without comment or criticism. There are no bad ideas in a brainstorm. Every activity, every suggestion is written down on a flip chart, white board, or other information-gathering surface where everyone in the group can see what's been offered.

Once all of the activities for the WBS are identified, team members can begin to weed out activities they perceive as superfluous to the effort. The head person reviews all of the activities and begins a secondary brainstorm to identify the missing activities through one of the techniques identified earlier. The same basic principles must apply. Ideas should not be criticized and *all* insights should be catalogued.

Crawford Slip

Many of the idea-generation tools available work under the premise that team members have an almost infinite amount of time. By contrast, the

Crawford Slip is extremely fast, efficient, and information-intensive. It is specially designed to gather large volumes of information in a very short time span.

Unlike a brainstorm, however, it does not promote synergy. Team members never have the opportunity to feed off one another's ideas. In the Crawford Slip, the facilitator gives each team member X number of Post-It® notes. X is determined by taking the anticipated number of activities in the project and multiplying by a factor of three or four. This allows for the inevitable overlap of activities identified by the team members.

Each team member is instructed to take a single Post-It® and to write on that note one specific work package seen as essential to the project. This can be broken down by function, by deliverable, by phase, or by any other measure the project manager deems productive. Once the team members identify an activity, the project manager instructs them to set that activity aside and move on to the next one. Every 30 seconds to one minute, each team member generates the name of yet one more work package on yet another Post-It®.

Once a sufficient number of activities is generated, the project manager determines whether it is appropriate to have the team work together to fill in the gaps (as described earlier) or if he/she will work independently to accomplish that goal.

Nominal Group Technique (NGT)

The nominal group technique is similar to the Crawford Slip in that the team has the opportunity to provide input in a non-synergistic approach. Unlike the Crawford Slip, however, team members do not generate a uniform number of activities and do not need to wait for their peers to add another work package to the list. In the nominal group technique, each team member is given a sheet of paper and told to list every identifiable work package. The individual results are then tabulated for group review and assessment. In conventional NGT, participants rank the results. In this situation, such a ranking would be moot, since the objective is not to identify the activities, but to ensure that as many activities as possible are identified.

Others

There are other idea generation techniques in the field. In the DeBono approach, for example, participants are asked to look at perspectives to encourage a broader understanding and higher level of participation. Participants are told to put on their "critic's hat" and their "supporter's hat" to emphasize differing attitudes and perspectives. In this situation, it might be appropriate to have team members use the "thinking hats" from a different angle. They could put on their "customer hats" and their "functional hats" and their "development phase hats" to collect insights on the different perspectives of the project.

For this and for the other techniques, simply alter the focus and the perspective to the work package level of the WBS.

Index

B

Bottom-Up Task-Oriented WBS, 20

C

Changes, 43
Checklist
    Bottom-Up Task Oriented WBS, 22
    Delphi Technique Applicability, 28
    Exit Interview Form, 50
    Gap Analysis - Consultant
    Validation, 30
    Gap Analysis - Delphi Technique, 28
    Gap Analysis - Networking
    Applicability, 24
    Gap Analysis - Networking
    Approach Success, 26
    Template WBS Construction, 37
    Top-Down Deliverable, 14
    Top-Down Task-Oriented WBS, 19
    Version Control, 47
Close-Out, 49
Construction Approaches
    Bottom-Up Task-Oriented WBS, 20
    Template, 31
    Top-Down Deliverable, 14
    Top-Down Task, 17

D

Definition, 1
Deliverable Orientation, 6

Advantages and Disadvantages, 6
Delphi Technique, 27

G

Gap Analysis, 23
    Consultant Validation, 29
    Delphi Technique, 27
    Networking, 23
    Template Comparison, 30

H

Hybrid Approaches, 38

I

Idea-Generation Techniques, 53

M

Mechanics, WBS, 5

N

Networking, 23
Numerical Sequencing, 5
    Deliverable Orientation, 6
    Task Orientation, 9

O

Orientation, 6
    Deliverable, 6

Task, 9
Orientation Checklist, 11

S

Storage and Retrieval, 51
    Keywords, 52

T

Task Orientation, 9
Template Construction, 31
        Sample Templates - References, 35
Template Construction Checklist, 37

Top-Down Deliverable Checklist, 16
Top-Down Task, 17
Top-Down Task-Oriented Checklist, 19

V

Version Control Checklist, 47

W

WBS Construction Approaches, 13